# Solastalgia

# Solastalgia

Brittney Corrigan

*for Courtney!*
*With great admiration*
*for your work.*
*2023*

JACKLEG PRESS

JackLeg Press
www.jacklegpress.org

ISBN: 978-1737513483

Library of Congress Control Number: 2022936417

Cover design: Jennifer Harris
Cover photo: Brin Levinson, *The Patriarch*
Author photo: Nina Johnson Photography

# Praise for *Solastalgia*

Growing up, Brittney Corrigan was, as she says, a real "snake child" and "horse girl," and though she didn't follow the path of her yearned-for careers as marine biologist or wildlife photographer, she became something just as necessary: a poet who tendrils the language of science with music, who stories the hard facts of the Anthropocene with poems that speak for the suffering lot of us— especially our nonhuman kin—as we struggle to survive this time. Here, then, is a book built from years of careful research and a loving attention to the living world. It is a book that I most need, one I will return to again and again as balm and guide, as an answer to the questions she poses in "Elegy for One Billion Animals": "What can we do to resurrect you? What on earth can we say?"

—Nickole Brown

These poems are a requiem for what is lost and what we're losing. They are also a rallying cry, refusing to erase the efforts of the many cries for climate justice ringing around the world.

—Camille Dungy

With the music of prayer and the precision of science, Brittney Corrigan has compiled a dazzling bestiary of the endangered and the everyday, from the backyard to the fossil record. Celebratory and mournful, audacious and tender, these astonishing poems offer a bold reassessment of what it means to be human in a time of climate crisis and mass extinction, a time when birdsong has become "no longer a chorus but a lonely, / indicating trill." Clear-eyed about what comes next, about what won't survive us and what will, *Solastalgia* nevertheless offers a stirring invitation to wonder, to hope, "to create / something beautiful from / the dissolution we have made." In an age of sweeping change and profound loss, Corrigan's expansive vision helps me imagine a way forward, a way to understand "how / the weight of loss can be beautiful / in its opening."

—Brian Simoneau

How can poetry speak to this moment of ecological unraveling and grief? Brittney Corrigan's collection, *Solastalgia,* is a brave and beautiful response to this call. In poems that sing with incantatory spells of direct address, Corrigan won't turn away from our burning world or from the miraculous embodiment of specific creatures we have lost or stand at the precipice of losing. With imagery grounded in science and soaring in imagination, these poems evoke the creatures they speak to, enacting their pulsating forms, their wrinkled snouts, fluttering wings, tufted ears, and whip-noted voices. This book is an "Anthropocene blessing" to all of us who yearn for ways to praise and pray and mourn in this teetering time.

—Anne Haven McDonnell

# Contents

Hydrosphere | Cryosphere

# Biosphere

# Clothesline for the Sixth Extinction

One end hitched to an iceberg's spire, the other looped
on the limb of a dragon tree, we string the cord across

oceans, continents, the grind of tectonic plates. Beneath,
we line up red rover-style, protest-style, arms linked

together, feet planted firm in the parched or flooded earth.
One of us holds a basket of pegs, another stands ready

to hoist and pin. When the animals come—some sprinting,
some barely able to lift flipper, paw, appendage, or fin—

our bodies collide with their bodies. We run our fingers
through manes and feathers, allow the many-legged to drum

at our skin. The line grows crowded with striped and spotted
pelts. We clip some by their tails, some by antler or wing.

They roar and screech until they settle in their dangling,
every eye turned toward the precipice. The horizon flares

at its edge. An elephant sways from its unironed trunk,
balanced by the massive teardrop of a whale, fluke fastened

toward the sky. They hang as hurricanes pummel, waters rise,
or wind whips the ground to blinding dust. We lean our heads

on each other's shoulders, clasp hands as we catch and catch.
The line bows, we secure each talon and claw again and again.

But there at the end, a small shift when our backs are turned.
A pair of hairstreak wings unlatches, disappears into the blue.

## The Strip Mall Changes Its Mind

At first, it took comfort in the scents from Body Beyond:
floral powders and cinnamon lotions mingled in the stuffy dim.

It watched over so many unfooted shoes. Bright dresses called out
in bold prints to suits in the dry cleaner's rack, still rows of ghosts.

Then the grief set in, the conveyer belt of Sushi Town twisted
like an empty gut. Its capillaries of people gone, quiet at the heart.

Undone, it hardly noticed windows shattering, walls crumbling
as trees limbed their way in. Sunlight on every rain-warped floor.

Missing the humans with their electric bodies, wires and pipes
spilled out between unmoved beams. Tireless beaks bored holes

in everything. But the moss was so soft. It made the unframing
bearable. Signs unlatched, bedded down in tendrilled leaves.

When the fox moved in, birthed two russet kits in a thicketed
shopping cart, wind like a breath, a sigh, rose past the splintered

rafters, the unlit lights. And so it happened: the forgetting. Painless,
its tender reclaiming. Dangling ceiling tiles sloppy with stars.

Canis

You think you want the puffball pooch
for your lap, or the gentle giant that lets
toddlers pull its ears. Or the hound trained
to bring back limp birds in its mouth:
refusing instinct, whistle-whipped, gorged
on praise. But the slender beast that roams
your streets at dawn and dusk has walked
this ground a million years. When wolves
and jackals landbridged their way out,
coyote stayed. Survived the poisons, bullets
fired from planes. Misunderstood, coyote
knows your nature. Slides between cars,
its muzzle full of mice. Come now. Doesn't
your heart wish to trot down darkened
sidewalks, outwit what has clobbered it,
yip and howl at every streetlight moon?
Here, come stand at the window. Watch
the yellow eyes, ears that swivel toward
the city's hum. This is the dog you've always
wanted. The one that turns city to wildscape.
Stops you in your tracks. Unguards your door.

## Opossum Nocturne

Perhaps it is poor night vision
that keeps us from seeing how you

preen our streets, devouring what
the sunlit crows have left behind.

We misunderstand your mouth,
crowded with keen-edged teeth

that dissect and undo the flesh
we are too squeamish, too unbrave

to carry with our human hands. We
should envy your thanatotic form, how

death visits you but then retreats. Why
do we not adore your prehensile tail,

how you dangle and brace and grip
like the acrobats we embellish

with sequins and tulle? The darkness
inside your pouch, the nyctophilic

eyes ripening within, should allure us
like the night sky we wish watched

over our city noise: the one so thick
with stars we're less blind for its light.

## Anthropocene Blessing: Corpse Flower

You who embarrass naturalists with your racy
scientific name—your coy and skirted spathe
unfolding in precocious maroon pleats
about your massive spadix, phallic offering
to the still-unscented air—how we tend
and wait years for you to bloom inside
our careful greenhouses, your wild kin
dwindling as the forests fall. How we revel
in your unapologetic stench, watch
the carrion beetles swarm toward your
tease of rotten meat and death. We hold
our noses but still lean in to see the mania
of insects do your bidding, smear their pollen
along rings of tiny flowers at your base.
May your corm be ever swollen. May your
inflorescence be ever graced by flies.
You who can warm your body to match
the heat of our own, may your odor outlast
us, we whose corpses feed the worms
below the wilting petals on our stones.

# Anthropocene Blessing: Black-Footed Ferret

Polecat of grasslands and sagebrush,
shrub steppe hunter of prairie dogs—
sliding undiscovered into burrows
to wring the like-sized creatures
as they sleep—in your arch-clawed,
nocturnal stealth, may you emerge
from underground not poisoned, not
plagued. May your orbicular ears
warn you of every rattlesnake
and hawk. May your soot-black
soles and banded eyes recall for us
our thieving nature, our territorial
ways. May our shadows on
the mounded ground not be raptorial.
May you not be relic. Not prey.

# Fear of Grasshoppers
### *Craig, Colorado (1980)*

Because of the legs bent backwards
and the bulbous eyes, the unpredictable
launch of their bodies into the summer
heat. Because of my girl-stick, nine-year-old
legs wading through the waist-high prairie
grass in a buzz of insect wings, the thwack
of their legs against my legs, the prairie
heat humming. Because the waist-high
grass stood between the house and the horses.
Because the gray horse, Stormy, lazed his liquid
eyes at me across the dry ranch grass, flicked
his tail and stamped at the gathering flies.
So many insect bodies, brown as the prairie
grass, wings a-whir by the dozens, slicing
my path to the horses, to the gray horse,
Stormy, tossing his mane in the heat. Their
alien eyes jumping into my running, their
backward-bent legs extending against
my skin, their antennae, their sectioned
abdomens, flinging themselves through
the grasses to bounce off my knees, my
feet crushing the insect bodies as I ran, the
sickening crunch and exoskeletal snap.

My hands splayed across my face, my
stick-legs hurdling through the springing
grasses, to the horses, the horses, the gray horse,
Stormy, quivering his hide in the heat.

# Horse-Girl

It's the smell coming off of them, the shimmering
ripeness, rich earth and animal heat. The way
her hand melts into their hides when she runs
her fingers along the sinews of their necks, the brown
bellow-pulse of their sides. It's the warm breath
from their soft nostrils, how it hovers around
her face and climbs through her hair. The sound
of the snorting and stamping, the way their manes
fall in coarse tendrils past their ears, the shiver
of their haunches alit with flies. The swish and slap
of their tails against her legs. Her legs crisp
and growing, she now stands as tall as their eyes,
she drapes her arms across their shifting backs.
She traces the muscles of their flanks, the knobs
of their fetlocks as she lifts and examines
their hooves, adjusts her boots. Their strong hips,
her strong hips, the toss of their heads, the toss
of her head, she swings herself astride them, takes up
handfuls of them, presses her young thighs into
the round girth of their sides. The ferocious, full speed
of their flying, their bodies rippling as one body, the rush
of the tussocks, oh, the sun as it comes down upon them
with ethereal thirst, it can't get enough of them, look at them,
swift and fierce and bursting with a need they cannot hide.

## Triolet for the Wildlife Photographer I Didn't Become

Eye to lens to animal eyes I wished to know:
wolves in winter, great cats lounging in the heat,
lone fox springing, diving for a rabbit in the snow.
Eye to lens to animal eyes I wished to know:
an owl's spin and blink, the intuition of a crow.
Earth and air and water where we'd meet,
my eye to lens to animal eyes I wished to know.
Just dogs in winter, house cats lounging in the heat.

## Oasis

Inside the veldt of your body:
a sphere of hurt. The dung beetle
that is your mind rolls it across
your chest, gathering the bitter
leavings, until it grows so large
you are pressed to the earth
with its weight. Lions stalk
your rib cage as it rises
and falls with your undoing.
Vultures, reverent in
their watch, wait for you
to succumb. What you didn't
expect was how the rough
tongues of the cats smooth you
to a sheen. When the baboons
move in around you, raucous
with their concern, you allow
them to groom. They pick each
nit from around your heart
until it is tender from their work,
beats loud enough to quiver
the dung ball to crumbs. You
thank the baboons, take their
faces between your hands. You

even thank the big cats, their
barbed tongues a necessary
kindness in the dusty heat
of the hungry world.

# Anthropocene Blessing: Black Rhino

You who are more likely than not
to die of a blow from your own kind—
one bicorned skull slamming into another,
the piercing of such thickened skin—
may the egrets and oxpeckers who feast
with their feet on your backs, devouring
parasites swollen with your solitary blood,
lift as you charge tree trunks and termite
mounds, turn crocodiles back into the mud.
May your horns, rough stalagmites between
your lily-folded ears, not be prized and poached
by we who are too much like you: so apt
to shake our heads and charge without
reckoning what it is we will gore.

## Anthropocene Blessing: Ghost Orchid

Little palm polly epiphyte, white frog
clinging to your pond apple, pop ash
trunks, pale roots tendrilling your green
root-body invisible. Profiled face an ashen
dragon drawing the swamp moths near—
streaked, fig, pawpaw, giant sphinx—
each tonguing your leafless, ethereal
throat. May your nectar spur, your thin
and papery bracts, spook all but the
hawkmoths who sup your sugar, drench
in your pollen all night. May you hover
unseen over every alligator eye, every
panther, every venomous snake. May
they serve as your unknowing guardians
against we who would muck through
tea-dark water, cypress trees limbing
our path, to steal your amphibious curls.
May you remain suspended, otherworldly.
Elusive and dangling, spectral-bright.

## Western Gray Squirrel Haibun

Telephone and internet wires stretch above the autumn street—
house to pole to house—threading through trees that could be
mistaken for forest. Branched bodies tower high enough to topple
chimneys, splinter roofs, if a strong wind barreled in and cracked
them down. Peregrine nest at a pinnacle of fir. Strew of pine cones
and needles beneath. Two gray squirrels—tails built for skywalking,
funambulist paws gripping the high wire—tightrope their way
through a din of crows that plunge and harass from either side.
Somewhere in the evergreens, a drey of sticks and moss. A scatter-
hoard of horse chestnuts and seeds. Clever acrobats, the ropewalking
squirrels chatter back at the black-beaked birds. When the peregrine
glides in, alights at the cross-top of a pole, the corvids shy back like
ghosts, and the rodents dart one way, then the other, suspended
between gutter and bough. One squirrel twists and scrambles, the
other loses footing and falls, tail hairs separating to catch the air. A
slowed parachuting to the street, body oriented to the earth, toes
spread and reaching for the ground. The falcon is content, this time,
to spectate: head swiveling slightly to catch the show.

balance of beings
gravity's center: the heart
held breath, fly or fall

## Raccoon Nocturne

You call us trash pandas—a name
that presumes we're drawn to the taste

of what you cannot stomach. We wash
what you waste, make it clean.

We were here first, before your boxy dens
and unsoft paths confused our foraging.

The trees in which we raised our kits
did not tremble with the noise of you

machining your way to work. Now,
we stare down your house cats until

they share their meals, reach our hands—
five-fingered and more perceptive

than your own—into their painted bowls.
You shout at us in the darkness, clatter

pots until we turn and flash our striped tails
as we scale your fences. But we are patient.

We will be awake long after you've slipped
into your flowered bedding, bamboo blankets,

pillows stuffed with the down of birds. All night,
our banded eyes will kindle your dreams.

## Invasive | Threatened

goat
kudzu
common carp
zebra mussel
water hyacinth
European starling
Northern Pacific sea star
cypress aphid, rosy wolfsnail
common rabbit, field mouse, nutria
sweet potato whitefly, black rat, wild boar
Asian long-horned beetle, Asian gypsy moth
chestnut blight, blackberry, salt cedar, apple snail
small Indian mongoose, bullfrog, cane toad, largemouth bass
gray squirrel, red fox, green crab, yellowjacket, brown tree snake
black wattle, hogweed, Nile perch, mesquite, leafy spurge, feral cat

Saddle-backed Rodrigues giant tortoise, white-throated ground Dove
South Island stout-legged wren, Higgins eye pearlymussel
small Mauritian flying fox, loach minnow, silver trout
San Martin Island woodrat, big-eared hopping mouse
bridled nail-tail wallaby, Yunnan lake newt
Southern marsupial mole, Guam broadbill
chestnut, red squirrel, Chatham bellbird
Hawaiian thrush, honeyeater
Attwater's prairie chicken
Mount Glorious day frog
Pacific madrone
Grevy's zebra
bog turtle
bushwren
elm

# Iteration

*after the Aldabra rail*

One flightless bird evolves twice, before and after extinction.
Collective bodies remember what it is to feel safe.

*You remember this, too. Before the world came lapping.*

A coral atoll—lagoon brimming with black-tipped sharks,
no people—flourishes. Giant tortoises wander between

turquoise worlds of sea and sky. The birds have no
reason to fly away. A body with no enemies simplifies.

*There was a time when you didn't need wings.*

Nothing is wasted. The birds push their long, ruddy necks
through the coastal grass. Nothing chases them down.

*There was a time when you never looked behind you.*

The first time the ocean takes the island, every species on it
goes extinct. A mass drowning. Thousands of years later,

the water recedes. Fossils and sand surface; flora blooms.
The bird's white-throated cousins land on the shores.

*There was a time when your throat was open to the sky.*

The bird evolves again. Again relinquishes its wings.
Again has no enemies. Again is a singular kind of being.

*You can do this, too. Sharks circle but can't cross land.*

Bodies remold. *Bodies wingless.* Bones tell stories. Versions
of stories. *You recolonize your body.* What it is to survive.

## Anthropocene Blessing: Pangolin

You who roll up in a Fibonacci
curl, keratin scales armoring your
mammalian skin. You of the delving
tongue, syruping termites and ants
into your toothless jaws. Burrower,
tree-swinger, long-distance swimmer,
you with your pangopup clinging
to the pine coned length of your tail.
Most-trafficked one, may the prehistoric
ball of your body not be lifted from
your grasslands, forests, woods. May
the fetal commas of your young not
stoke our hunger or desire. May your
peripheral, black-marble eyes, your
curving claws, untuck from your
spiraling form. May you lumber,
bipedal, to where you could
outnumber us, your one defense
to shelter in place until the world
gives up and gets out of your way.

## Anthropocene Blessing: Giant Panda

You of the contrasting pelt,
the great, white moon of your
face broken by the swathing
black of your shadowed eyes.
Living fossil, solitary in your
Sichuan world, may your
folivorous hunger be sated
by abundant bamboo. May
you sit back on your ursine
haunches, noble and rotund,
and munch an infinite
columnar feast. May the tiny
pink culm of your cub
grow into its ying-yang form.
May you flourish like
the shoots and canes: rooted,
reforested. No diplomats.
No cultural exchange.

# Lithosphere

## $pecimen BHI 3033: $tan

Once a pelvis surfacing in the cliffs of Hell Creek,
once a titan among gingko and redwood trees,

once a survivor of broken ribs, broken neck, gored
skull. *T. rex* under the hammer—nearly all original

bones, massive head perfectly preserved—skeleton
of meticulous assemblage stalking the auction block.

As the numbers rise, as anonymous dollars mount,
bone-ghosts sigh in castings from museum floors,

paleontologists clench and wring empty hands. Bids
tower over the sale of Sue: *T. rex* once embalmed

in a seasonal stream, once riddled with parasitic bites.
Sue of the much-studied skull, the beloved wishbone.

Stan of the 65-million-year-old skeleton, final price tag
half his age. Remains recast in nonscientific worth.

Fossil of fury, Stan of the private collection, vanished
beast, *T. rex* reburied, monster of going, going, gone.

# Fossil Record: Smilodon

As a child, I put my hand between its teeth,
dropped coins down its throat to make it roar.

Pillared in the museum lobby: open-jawed
bust of a saber-toothed cat, not a Sphinx

but a Cerberus guarding the fossilized
dead. Through rooms of wire-strung bones

and taxidermied beasts, I was drawn to
dioramas like a light-mired moth, pressing

the buttons to hear their worlds described
in tinny voices limned with prehistoric

lore as I held the bulky headphones
tighter to my human ears. This felid,

scalpel-mouthed and fierce, once stalked
giant sloths. Once was taken by the tar pits,

bubbling cuspids, thick with tusks and fangs.
Once, snarling dire wolves watched the stuck

cat yowl. How I could hear the ghost-growls
echo through museum walls, each fossil-body

rigid with the sound. Small mammal that I was,
pennies in my pocket as the exit loomed.

## Anthropocene Blessing: Monkey Puzzle Tree

Piñonero, living fossil, umbrellaing
ambassador for your country though she
has burned you, leveled you for fleecy herds,
cleaved your pyramidal body to build bridges,
boats, and beams. May your reptilian,
symmetrical branches bear your pollened cones
into the temperate wind. May the triangular
scales of your leaves beanstalk themselves
into a clarity of air. May your seeds find
the tender-jointed paws of the long-haired
grass mouse, who, in its russet efficiency,
will bury and disperse. May you germinate,
may your thousand-year, spreading roots tap
the volcanic soil. May your spiny trunk
safeguard its calyxed rings. May you resist
the fires that will consume us, cast off
your anthropoid name. You who sheltered
prehistoric beasts, may you confound.

# Proof

*"An animal can only die once, and when it does, there's a
vanishingly slim chance that it will become a fossil... While it's
alive, though, a creature can stamp proof of itself all across the
landscape."*
          —Atlas Obscura *(November 27, 2019)*

Spectral in the salt crust,
footprints of mammoths—
round and wide as the lid
of a garbage can—surface
in the gypsum dust. Once
submerged in sediment,
crook-clawed imprints
of a ground sloth's feet
emerge beside the familiar
shapes of human soles.
Scientists kneel and point
radar machines at ghosts.
Before our swooshed
and rubber-bound
heels and toes walked
across this roiling planet,
before the loofahed skin
of our ball mounds
shunned the layers of soil
between the webbed
dactyls of our feet—
Pleistocene groundwater

upwelled in the arid
earth, locked tracks
of ancient travelers in.
Mammoth prints muddle
human ones. Human
footprints crisscross
the circular dents
of mammoth feet.
As sands shift, trace fossils
rise into the landscape,
disappear again beneath
the dunes, while
on a city sidewalk
a child presses her hand
into a square of cooling
concrete, carves
her initials carefully
next to her thumb.

# Fossil Record: Dimetrodon

I claimed the spine-sailed monster as my own, balled
my tiny fists around its plastic forms—primary reds
or blues then—not these life-like replicas, incongruous
beside the blind-boxed anime figurines that
line my children's shelves. *Dimetrodon,* named for two
measures of teeth in its slope-curved jaw, neural
vertebrae anchored in its muscular back. Each
ascending bone suggests the crosshatch of a fish. Years
later I would learn it's not a dinosaur at all. Cisuralian
beast, extinct some 40 million years before orders
of reptiles evolved to rule the Earth. Less reptile
than mammal—synapsid—not mammal, not reptile.
What manner of creature might I be, then, if
my children think me one thing—Garanimal
mother of bright, simple hues—but another
woman rises up, window-skulled, manifold and new?

## Anthropocene Blessing: Orangutan

Person of the forest, you whose skeleton
is shaped for aboreal life, you of the curved
fingers and toes, you fist walker, you
with your suspensory hook grip. May
your rufous hair center you like the sun.
May the fruit you hold to your long-calling
mouth be a planet from which you suckle.
May you cast the orb-rind into the understory
and swing your star-flare limbs across
each gap. May the nests you build nightly
hammock you away from us, we who flatten
your trees for our many oils. In this growing
darkness, may your titian bodies
be the only lights that burn.

# Elegy for One Billion Animals

We can say to ourselves you didn't suffer, but the truth
is a lick of flame climbing a brittle tree. Suffering is
the charred husks of bristlebirds. The singe of koala fur.

We can say it was only lightning at fault, but the truth
falls like ash. Wishing it were water, we wade ankle deep
in what remains, what skink and frog bodies have become.

We can say we'll help you who have survived. We drop
carrots and sweet potatoes from the sky into wallaby paws.
Heat so thick it pulsates. No telling smoke from ghosts.

Little pouched ones, you mortal convoys scurrying
from the flames. If only we could turn out our pockets
and find you whole. We can say we'll carry you:

scoop up you withered dunnarts and quokka, greater gliders
with your smoldering tails. Your black eyes like embering
coals as we wrap what's left of you in the shirts off our backs.

But oh, honeyeater. Glossy cockatoo. Your nests exploding
suns as you lift and find no haven in the blackened air.
What can we do to resurrect you? What on earth can we say?

# Lahar

*for Mount Rainier*

> *"It is not easy to be this small and live in your shadow."*
> —*Naomi Shihab Nye, "Negotiations with a Volcano"*

Here in the subduction zone, plates collide
into Earth's mantle beneath my feet, and

I know this ghosting town will be smothered if
you crack and roar. What's buried in the cemetery

will be further buried. The century-old tavern
will buckle and splay, you'll choke the lake

with pyroclastic debris. Viewed from above,
your glaciers radiate, corolla-whorled

in their flare: *Ohanapecosh, Mowich, Emmons,
Sarvent, Muir.* Your flanks firm in ice until

the heat at your heart melts all to furious flow,
and we in your path return to dust and ash.

But for now, let me wander in your unnamed
snowfields. Let me startle marmot and pika

from your boulders and trees. Let the mountain
goats, sure-footed and brave, ascend in the frigid

air. Let what's molten be pacified, contained.
Let the ground be wildflowered, unabrased.

# Carpe Diem

Forget the day—how hours flatten the way rising water turns islands back to sea, how minutes tire of treading and flail their tentacled fingers above the surface, grasping at gull legs, the mired rim of a trash vortex, anything to hold on to before seconds turn blue from the effort and the whole mess siphons down—yes, forget the day, in terms of this planet—a planet that has been here 4.5 billion years—our existence but a fraction of a percent, a blip even to the dinosaurs that tromped and scrabbled themselves across the Earth's crust one hundred and fifty-nine million years longer than we've been digging our toes in the sand, swinging from branches, praising the soil or stewarding the land or unrocking the mountains or replacing redwoods with skyscrapers or talking about the weather or generally fucking everything up, yes, this isn't about the day anymore, it's about reach out and grab that ice shelf—don't let that big white bear and her two black-eyed cubs float away—*carpe Ursus maritimus, carpe Pongo abelii*—orangutans grooming their 97%-identical-to-human-genome-selves in the rainforests, please *carpe* the rainforests—*carpe Panthera pardus orientalis, carpe Panthera tigris sondaica*—big cats in their patterned fur coats, in their slink-vanishing away from us—*carpe Balaenoptera musculus*—whale shark circling our dreams, vesseling its way through our paintings and poems—*carpe Thaumatibis gigantean*, giant ibis—the world's most endangered and evolutionarily distinct bird—*carpe Adelocosa anops*, Kaua'i cave wolf spider that doesn't spin webs, that chases down its prey the way we are chasing our own tails now, digging ourselves a meteor-sized crater of a grave, exponentially expanding daily what we'll take down with us, dragging the aurora borealis and its tundra and permafrost after us, yes, forget the day, *carpe* the last of the dark sky places, the quietest places on Earth, the deserts with their nocturnal rhythms—flora and fauna that know what it is to survive—yes, forget the day, *carpe noctis, carpe noctis*—let there be stars when we seize the last of the light.

# Anthropocene Blessing: Sumatran Tiger

*Panthera tigris*, you whose sister species
have already vanished from your Island
of Gold. Broad-striped hunter of wild
pigs, tapir, mouse-deer—their blood
on your medicinal canines, erupting
into the ruff of your tropical fur. You
who retreat on dewclawed, silent paws
to where the subcanopy is thick,
the forest's ancient core, though our
plantations of palm oil and acacia
ooze in from every side. May you,
at the center, radiate in your molten
pelt, burnished haunches balanced
on the backbone slopes of your volcanic
forest floor. May your tail switchback
away from us like a viper. May your skull
be ever mantled in your patterned skin.
May we whose hearts are igneous
with disdain not swallow tiger wine
nor powder your bones. May the magma
of your heart never harden, never cool.

## New Year's Eve in the Anthropause

Let us stay home with our sparklers and our peaceful dogs.
Let us watch the ball drop in a quiet, empty square.

Let the geese stroll on the tarmac. Let no machines take wing.
Let the wild turkeys strut and assemble in Harvard Yard.

Let us stay home with uncorked bottles and cats on our laps.
Let us wave to each other from our individual screens.

Let the Japanese sika deer walk Nara's templed streets.
Let the wild boar ramble through towns in Italy and Spain.

Let us stay home with our slow-cooked black-eyed peas.
Let us binge on TV, watch movies with our gangly teens.

Let the pumas roam in Santiago, the jackals in Tel Aviv.
Let the whales sing in unboated waters, the birds in noiseless air.

Let us stay home with unraveling marriages, with dispirited kids.
Let us put our exhaustion to bed early. Tuck in our worries and fears.

Let us turn out the lights, let the loggerhead turtles come ashore.
Let us sleep in this world of our making. Let us rise and remake.

## Ghost Town

The roads open

       as if they are mountain trails

meandering

       over the horizon

and the traffic lights

       are bright birds

swinging

       on the air

and the shuttered buildings

       might as well be stone—

how long until they go

       mossy with our absence—

we could turn out the dogs

    ask them to find

what we need out there

    and bring it home


but they would feel the quiet

    spaces expanding in their bones

shake their pelts

    take off across meadowed parking lots


and run—

## Anthropocene Blessing: Baobab

You of the wide, cylindrical trunk,
too large for any embrace, your
tufts of towering branches threaded
with nests. You of watermelon-scented
flowers, snouted by fork-marked lemurs
through the star-curtained night.
You whose seed-dispersers are already
ghosts, elephant birds lost to the dust
centuries ago, leaving you yearning
many centuries hence. May thirst
never topple you. May lightning
never split your fibrous core. May
your crown reach palmate leaves
into the vast blue heat. Tree of Life,
may you bear fruit despite how
we have failed you. Your taproots
reaching for water beneath our feet,
we with your citrus-bright gifts
upon our lips, may you outlast us.
May you who are sacred and innocent
shed us like dry leaves and remain.

# Atmosphere

## My Eco-Anxiety and Solastalgia Have It Out

If the ocean rises over me while I sleep.
*Before the whaling ship and garbage barge.*

If the volcano I can see from the supermarket erupts.
*Where the tree line ends, the caldera and the lake.*

If Cascadia fractures and falls into the sea.
*Fir and spring water. Understory. Crown of leaves.*

If The Big One hits and I can't get to my children.
*Open spaces. What's a smokestack? A crane is a bird.*

If hurricanes flatten and flood places I've not yet been.
*Manatees in the mangroves, no ship-stricken skin.*

If the sea ice melts and the polar bears float away.
*A blue iceberg is the compression of pure snow.*

If there are no more bees.
*Fields of wildflowers. Honey in the mouths of bears.*

If the plants and animals all die.
*Dogs are descended from gray wolves. Wild blueberries on a hill.*

If it's just so hot. If it's just so cold.
*Skinny-dipping in the quarry. Snowball fights until dusk.*

If wildfires never stop burning.
*Aspen leaves in autumn. Sagebrush keeps company with rabbits and elk.*

If the sky turns red.
*Sunrises in the desert. Sunsets on the coast.*

If scientists plead into a void.
*When I stand beneath the stars and weep.*

## L'Appel du Vide

Carefully, with a pair of kid-size scissors I borrow
from my child's art supplies, I snip each round
opening in the six-pack yoke, imagine the sea

creatures I'm sparing. Turtles whose leathery
necks won't bulge and split but will tuck neatly
back into their shells. When I think of us

here together in our swing around the sun—
our floods and fires, our stores of coal and oil,
the distance we put between us and those we hate,

our fondness for small, furred things and light
through trees and standing at the ocean's edge,
the distance we close between us and those we love—

it all feels like a blur, the round rock of our world
chasing a darkness that expands and expands
and expands. When faced with dizzying

heights, our human selves imagine jumping—
off the roof of a building, a bridge, a cliff.
But mostly we don't jump. Mostly we step back,

invincible. We retract our fear inside us, shell
our hearts. No wonder we hurtle our way through
extinction after extinction, grazing the edge.

Standing in my kitchen, holding the severed rings
as they dangle and twist, kelp-like, over the bin,
I imagine the world without us, think how we

are staring down the void, barely able to resist
its existential call. Every other living thing on Earth
watches us, wishes we would hurl ourselves in.

# Dogs of Chernobyl

Exclusion zone of radioactive dogs
    Alsatian   mongrel   brindle   merle   patch

no more buses   no shot carcasses
    guards and checkpoints   abandoned ruins

sarcophagus-shadowed
    wolf-wooded   red-forested   ice-kissed

lean in the unpeopled haven   dogs of the rewilding
    Przewalski's horse   bison   moose   lynx   bear

roe deer   red deer   wild boar   beaver   badger   fox
    white snow   regreened leaves   dogs of the fallout dust

# Vanishing

*Nearly one-third of the wild birds in the United States and Canada have vanished since 1970, a staggering loss that suggests the very fabric of North America's ecosystem is unraveling.*
            –The New York Times *(September 19, 2019)*

As the world's cities teem
with children—flooding
our concrete terrains with shouts
and signs—as the younglings balance
scribbled Earths above their heads,
stand in unseasonal rain
or blistering sun,

the birds quietly lessen
themselves among the grasslands.
No longer a chorus but a lonely,
indicating trill: Eastern meadowlark,
wood thrush, indigo bunting—
their voices ghosts in the
chemical landscape of crops.

Red-winged blackbirds veer
beyond the veil. Orioles
and swallows, the horned lark
and the jay. Color drains from

our common home so gradually,
we convince ourselves
it has always been gray.

Little hollow-boned dinosaurs,
you who survived the last extinction,
whose variety has obsessed
scientific minds, whose bodies
in the air compel our own bodies
to spread and yearn—
how we have failed you.

The grackles are right to scold us,
as they feast on our garbage
and genetically-modified corn.
Our children flock into the streets
with voices raised, their anger
a grim substitute
for song.

## The Last Two Northern White Rhinos Discuss the Birds and the Bees

The Kenyan sun is sinking, round yellow fruit
in a sky stained purple and red. *Fatu, my daughter,*

says Najin—her horns beginning to silhouette
like the whistling acacia trees, flies leavetaking

from her thick, gray skin—*are you feeling well again,*
*after the harvesting?* Fatu's backside is sore, her belly

still hollow. *Mother,* she says, *I wish I could carry*
*the next of us the way you carried me. Will they*

*sculpt my calf from mud? Fasten on ears of diamond*
*euclea leaves?* Najin lowers her wrinkled snout

to the cooling earth, considers her answer through
a mouthful of grass. Watches the guards patrolling

with long, bright guns. *They will make another of us*
*with frozen ghosts,* says Najin. She misses Suni

and Sudan, the smell of their hides in the equatorial
heat. *Our southern sisters will carry the new ones*

*for us. The new ones will be planted like seeds.*
Olive baboons call out from the edge of night.

*Mother,* says Fatu. *I will watch for them at the horizon.*
She imagines their bodies building like clouds for a storm.

# Anthropocene Blessing: Monarch Butterfly

Milkweed, common tiger, wanderer.
You of the poison-filled body,
citrine hues of your wings framed
in obsidian—flutter of stained-glass
membranes alighting on asters, thistles,
goldenrod. May your banded
instars devour their white-sapped
hosts: antelopehorn, heartleaf,
woolly, whorled. May you find
on your long migration every
waystation, each garden clumsily
raised by human hands. May you
overwinter free of herbicides
from our modified, resistant crops.
May you not fly headlong into
our windshields and grilles. May
your singular, pearly eggs shelter
on the undersides of soft-furred
leaves, survive to pupate, j-hang,
shed their chrysalis-revealing
skins. May your metamorphosis
be a lesson for we who are slow
to change. We who cannot
seem to figure how to create
something beautiful from
the dissolution we have made.

# The Ghost of Marlin Perkins Visits Me Wearing a Copperhead

The kind of snake that almost bit my father when he was a boy,
draped around Marlin's shoulders and braceleting his ashen arms.

*Do you remember,* he asks, *how our cameras showed the predator
make the kill? How you'd root for the cheetah, no matter how pitiful*

*the gazelle?* And I do. Blood was the truth of it. Prides of lions
muzzle-deep in bright entrails. Claws to muscle, teeth to bone.

*When I was a zookeeper,* he tells me, *I curated the herpetarium.
Cottonmouths, Gaboon vipers, blue racers from my Missouri home.*

And I know. I was a snake child, too. My fourth grade teacher
kept a rattler in her basement, let me hold the gentle corn snake

she brought to show our class. I hunted wild garter snakes
in prairie-dogged fields. Fed them on minnows and worms.

*You know,* he says, lifting the copperhead off his spectral neck,
one hand still gripped firm behind its triangular head, *we never*

*did find that Yeti, Sir Edmund and I. What do you imagine is out there
in the world, that we haven't yet seen?* I think of the depths of oceans,

shy crowns of trees, small insects nearly invisible to the human eye.
And I want to respond, but then the wolves start up, their voices wild

in the kingdom of the dark. *Ah*, he says, *they're calling me back.*
As Marlin turns to go, the copperhead loosens, darts its tongue

through the notch of its lips, readies its venomous fangs. And I
can't help but be riveted, waiting for the animal instinct of its bite.

# Peatland Aisling

*They've taken the skeleton*
*Of the Great Irish Elk*
*Out of the peat, set it up*
*An astounding crate full of air.*
—Seamus Heaney, "Bogland"

*and I rose from the dark,*
*hacked bone, skull-ware,*
*frayed stitches, tufts,*
*small gleams on the bank.*
—Seamus Heaney, "Bog Queen"

In the dream, Heaney's bog queen comes leathered
and fox-curled, saxifrage-ringed and riding the bones

of a giant deer. Within its prehistoric antlers, short-eared
owls swivel tufted heads and stare. Hen harriers circle

blue-gray bodies against a grayer sky. Where the great beast
steps, orchids bloom. Around the coffin bones of its feet,

a flock of curlews whistles and darts. The bog queen opens
a mummied fist, a dozen hares rushing from her fingers,

sprinting into wintergreen and heath. Her voice long gone—
a ghost light in the buttery bog—I hear its changeling plead

in the otter-slick gloom. Ache and branching of my heart
into sphagnum moss as the bone deer stoops to graze.

The peatlands sigh and syrup carbon from the air, absorb
my breath. And the bog queen's hands turn to pipewort,

her sternum to a merlin's breast, a collarbone of wings.
The bog keeps what it keeps and we take what we take.

From the bog queen's darkened skull, a whooper swan.
Skeletal deer disassembling. Peat soaking me to the bone.

## En Plein Air

Painter with horse-hair brush in a field of mustangs,
animal-bodied palette at hand: carmine red for sunset,

blush of cochineal insects plucked from prickly pear.
Sepia sky ombrés through cloud canvas to plain, cuttlefish

ink staining dusty hides, restless fetlocks that shift weight
in summer's post-storm light. Bloom of tufted cirrus clouds

in an eggshell streak above the ridge. Mares' manes fall
along muscled crests, cirri in bone black and mummy

brown. Nicker and brushstroke. Stamp and blend.
Ring of hooves and flanks in twilit hue. Dapple

gray and pinto, rush of wind through painter's smock.
Blue roan, cremello, chestnut, buckskin. Painter's skin

copper-red in the lengthening dusk. Fall of Tyrian purple
across muzzles and flanks, color crushed or milked

from murex snails—elongate, sea-salted shells sculptured
with spines—tinted by crepuscular light. Mirage of painter,

dream of horses, now dissipate into bluebunch, wheatgrass,
muhly, wild rye. Feral pigmentation in the prairie night.

# Kulning

The sound is a woman standing in the pleats
of the mountain's summer skirts, her throat

haunted by sister-elders calling back
a hundred seasons, a hundred more.

Each morning, the cows vanish into rocky folds.
Days of brooms and needlework and cheese.

There are no men, and the women can be
tender and loud. The spine of cliffs shivers,

amplifies the lilting spell. The women call
to each other, call to their hearkening herds.

The women are loud. The children must
cover their ears as they stand at the source.

There are wolves, but the wolves know
the meaning of songs that carry for miles.

There are bears, but they only lift
their heads and sway. The lynx swivel

their tufted ears and spindle back the way
they came. The women are loud, and

the wayfaring cattle trundle their gentle
bodies home, bells a tin echo twined

in each lyricless phrase. The forest darkens,
and the kine accumulate like summoned

ghosts. The women's voices ornament
the alpine air. The women are loud.

Their voices toll and toll. The mountains
swell and cower with the sound.

## Orion in the Oregon Outback

Even the silence is swallowed by the dark.
December sky an impenetrable cast of stars,
but still the brightest forges anchor the map.

Shouldering red and blue giants, Orion hunts
as I watch from the playa's edge, Winter Ridge
a shadow, a second darkness at the horizon's rim.

Coyotes call into the black span of night, staccato
yip-howls sparring with the greater and lesser dogs
at Orion's heels. And I imagine the hunter turning

his head to look back at his hounds, nebular chiton
swiveling about his knees as he quiets their animal
alarm. But it is too late. The she-bear and her cub

are already making for the milky swath of luminous
and dark matter where I now fix my eyes, which brim
from the biting cold and the thought of leaving this vast

and wild place when the sun's golden horses wake
and hasten across the lakebed. But for now, I watch as
Orion—earthborn and heavenbound, great slayer of beasts,

hunter of every animal that exists—lays down his sword
at the feet of the northern sky's queen. Hooks his thumbs
in his belt and tilts his head up, as I do, to take in the stars.

# Anthropocene Blessing: Nightjar

Little goatsucker, bugeater,
you with moth bodies fluttering
their final moments in your bill.
You of the long, bark-mottled
wings. You of the broad-leafed
woods. In your crepuscular forays,
may each ghostling insect vanish
within your bristle-whiskered beak.
May the speckled eggs you lay
on the unnested leaf litter incubate
invisibly from mongeese, from
the jaws of feral cats. May you
distract our urban eyes from where
your cinnamon-downy chicks
fledge in the understory
by lifting your vibrating form
in conspicuous flight. Little
nighthawk, may your whip-noted
voice infiltrate the limestone
world. Tucuchillo, may your
metallic song be a knife ascending
in the darkness, protecting your
thorny thickets from the forest
mulcher's spinning slice.

# Tweet

As global temperatures ratchet up,
a female zebra finch sings to her eggs.
Embryonic chicks take note,
orchestrate their bodies to ratchet down.
Hatchlings grow into smaller birds:
easier to keep cool, less energy
for flight. Earth incubates
in its atmospheric shell.
The sun warbles on.

# Laika

*after the Soviet space dog of Sputnik 2 (1957)*


Frightened, we shove things before us into the world.

decoy
>> subject
>>>> shield

Sometimes beings, hearts tripling in pace.
Panting.
Breath expiring as the monster overhangs.

The canary's song
dwindles
in the darkness of the tunnel's cold bones.

Small animals
carry tumors on their backs until we're certain
we understand.

The little dog in her spacesuit
remembered how the streets were lean.

How she ran in a pack, chasing down
the hobbled and the weak.

How she barked until her name became that barking.

Her body circled and circled
the Earth, which still held us.
Circled and circled, the way dogs do
when they're trying to lie down.

## Rabbit, Rabbit, Rabbit

The night a neighbor girl knocks on our door,
baby rabbit in the bowl of her hands, I place

it in a darkened box of straw, know it won't
make it to morning. My grandmother's tradition

for the first day of each month: stand at the edge
of the bed upon waking, make a wish, yell

*Rabbit! Rabbit! Rabbit!* and jump. Tiny rabbit
body in my palm, soft and cold and still.

Rabbit sitting on the moon, pestling herbs
for the gods. A chant of white or gray rabbits

to ward off smoke. The Black Rabbit of Inlé:
his taking of this small life, his taking of my

grandmother when I was still small. I must
give this little un-rabbit back to the ground.

Oh, to be so frightened that your heart cannot
go on. But first, I must wake my young child.

On this first of the month, I ease tangles
separate through my hands. Sense something

quivering just beneath what's real as I leave
the room. From down the hall, I hear

the bedframe sigh. Little undone heart cupped
in my hands. Little voice shouting a herd

of rabbits onto the floorboards. I hop
from foot to foot as they run past.

## Doraphobia

*(fear of the fur and skin of animals)*


Her hands on the steering wheel blanch and grip,
trees on either side of the road stitched with wild

noise louder than her skid-stopped car. She imagines
the grille, twisted beneath the hood's crumple and hiss,

shuts her eyes against what must be pocked
with bloodied hair and hide. The deer has not risen,

has not bounded nor staggered into the mourning
woods. As a child, school field trips to the zoo

rendered her immobile—face pressed to the cement
walls of underwater viewing caves, heart frozen

at the thought of polar bear paws and their paddle
of white fur, or the slick gray pelts of seals—

as her classmates cawed and clamored against the glass
for a closer look. She could smell the dust and dung

rippling from elephant skin, sense leopard haunches stalking
her with their scatter of spotted eyes. The road shrinks now,

light sunsetting and no other cars for miles. Pinned to her seat
like the animal body pressed to the pavement, she tries to recall

the sound of her children breathing. Perhaps when she finally
gets out of the car, steadies herself and rounds the buckled frame,

the doe will resemble a sleeping child. And she could do this.
She could kneel beside the still-warm face as if it were only

fevered, a creature of her own making she could soothe and mend.
She could close its terrified eyes with the smallest touch.

## Os Sacrum

Your bones in the foxglove meadow—
disarrayed by animal mouth or human
touch—summer bones, clean bones,
sun-baked bones, scattered bones
no longer bound in the shape of you—
mule deer I crouch beside in your skeletal
rest—unbodied in this riversound meadow,
bees weaving in and out of your holed
bones, holy bones, unwhole bones,
speckled stalks of watchful flowers
keening in the meadow-shushed wind.
I take your sacrum bone in my hand—
sacred bone, bone of spine base, bone
of pelvic nest, bone of hipped wings—
run my fingers over smooth channels,
sacral crest, sacral canal, bony ridges,
sacral promontory, notch my thumbs
beside the bone rise, bony fin. I should
leave this bone here—quiet home
to sing your skeleton to sleep, foxglove
thrilling out of bone—but I love the weight
of it in my hand, the press of my thumbs
at the lip of each foramen, meadow bone,
deer bone, calling to the bones beneath
my skin. And so I carry this bone, your bone,

os sacrum, sacred bone, away from
your ghost body, deer ghost, scattered
ghost, ghost bone, bone of bees, bone I lift,
animal I lift and feel the running.

## Anthropocene Blessing: California Condor

King of birds, you of the nine-foot wingspan,
you who glide for hours on currents of air
without a single beat, thousands of feet above
the leaden earth. Scavenger ancestor, only
surviving member of your genus, longest-lived.
May you feast on the flesh of the dead
as you toss their spirits up to the sky. May
the carrion ghosts look down upon your
unplumaged head, your black-feathered,
sacred form, and be healed of all that stalked
them in this world. May you be not poisoned
by our buckshot, seething in each carcass
we leave behind. May you outgrow our
captivity to hatch your single eggs in mountain
cliff caves, giant redwood trees. New World
vulture, may your bulbous, wrinkled visage
remember how you soared over mammoths.
May you be revered as virtuous, as rising back
from the brink, as gathering your flock around
the fallen. May you take death in your mouth
and find it sweet, find that it sustains.

# Hydrosphere | Cryosphere

# Crow Opus

What may we take between worlds when
our bodies un-nest, when the tiny boats
of our hearts falter and capsize? Does
the soprano's song settle in the shell
of her skull or feather out across the expanse
of blue? Do the beekeeper's charges follow
her into the dark, or the light? Do the nurse's
caregiving hands, now turned to ash, still
buoy up those she's tended and healed?

Crow messengers scold us daily for
wasting their gifts. They try to tell us: you
are not bound here. Husks of small beings
contain the whole ladder of life's unfolding.
Fine-worn beach glass tells us all we need
know about time, and how it smooths.
Each shiny trinket is the ordinary made
brighter; each ribbon, a path to untangle
with the toil of our wrinkling hands.

We feel the half-century tiding in our bones,
which belong to us and to the planet's roil
and tilt. The crows assemble in their familiar
listening, hearing not only the murmur
of grasses in wind and the purpling drain

of sky into brine. They tip their sleek heads
toward our longing for each other, and for
what we have lost. They show us: look how
the sea brings back everything, but changed.

# Age Old

In my waning gibbous face, as the wrinkles take hold
of my skin, I think of the frilled shark—living fossil—

collar of gills beneath its jaws, throat a scaffold
of fringe, trident-toothed, slender body in the deep.

My mouth, teeth still my own, but at the threshold
of my lips, just a hint of tortoise-pucker, fine furrows

on the wizened upper rim. And oh, the roothold
of expressions: laugh lines, frown lines, crow's feet

that recall prehistoric kin. Soon, when gravitational folds
sag where my body loved the sun, I will praise elephants:

their bodies gentle and fierce, pleats and creases manifold
and much-caressed. And here at my forehead, where curls

are silvering, I thrill and wish for them a thousandfold—
loops of white, whorls of gray—immortal jellyfish

of luminous tendrils that my fingers twine and enfold,
press to my palm: life line, fate line, heart line, mount of moon.

## Triolet for the Marine Biologist I Didn't Become

My land-limbs twined and woven in the deep
with bodies flippered, tentacled, and finned.
Remora-like, my heart's barnacled keep.
My land-limbs twined and woven in the deep
among the upright whales, plumbed in their sleep.
Beside the walrus, seamed and thickly skinned.
My land-limbs twined and woven in the deep.
Geared body flippered, tentacled, and finned.

# Anthropocene Blessing: Blue Whale

May your automobile-sized
heart, pulsing in the chassis
of your massive, floating form,
claim a new comparison,
one not skeletoned of
plastic and steel, profuse
with oil, but deserving
of your fringed and sieving
jaws, the reach of your
resonant moans. May you
always be the largest,
the longest lived. Leave us
treading, exhausted
in your wake.

# Anthropocene Blessing: Sea Turtle

You of the precious-scuted carapace,
your mosaiced flippers crescenting
the water as you dive for jellyfish
and decapods— creatures of abundant
tentacles and many legs. You who mow
the sea grass carpeting the ocean floor,
who carry your breath along the tourmaline
beds. May your serrated beak never know
plastic or bycatch, never press against
the polyamide weave of nets. When
you haul ashore, may you snow-angel
the sand for your clutch, may your
soft-shelled eggs huddle unnoticed,
untouched. May your untended hatchlings
outrun every seabird and fox. May
the reptilian pools of their eyes be graced
by darkness, save the glowing wave-line
that beckons them from nest to ocean's tug.
May their fleeing shells upend the night.

# Cephalopods Have Three Hearts

Inkless in the deep,
the vampire squid flares the web
of its spiny cloak.

Emitting blue light,
the firefly squid coaxes fish
into lustrous arms.

Our darkened dreams spin
in the eyes of the giant:
we are mere ghost ships.

...

Cuttlefish see no
color. Sepia ink and
blue-green blood—just light.

And as to its skin:
chameleons of the sea.
Color, pattern, hue.

Then, the cuttlebone:
a crystalline body-boat.
We see you. We don't.

...

Octopus, making
of most anything a door.
Limbs, siphon, beak, eyes.

Two hearts for the gills,
another for the body.
Soft. More blood than bone.

We of only one
heart cannot fathom how you
must die for your young.

# Slow Living

On the days when I am beaming at the list
of things I've accomplished before noon—a run,
a shower, breakfast (two sorts) for my children,
breakfast (another sort) for myself, email, dishes,
tending to cats and dogs—I wonder at the algal
bodies of three-toed sloths, how they barely
have need to move, everything within reach.
Or the garden snail—one-footed and sure-footed—
a single leaf in the rain enough of a world.
Starfish and anemones—patient and bright—
wait for sustenance to come to them.
In the span of an afternoon when I have cleaned
and telephoned and problem solved and likely
cried, a giant tortoise has grazed and napped,
basking in the sun. By the time I've cooked dinner
(hopefully just one sort) and helped the children
with homework, folded laundry, checked items
off lists, herds of manatees have rested, munched
on water grasses, rested some more. Undressing
at last for a well-earned six hours of (likely
interrupted) sleep, I imagine a slow loris
just waking up to sit in stillness, large eyes
reflective in the dark, biding time with its toxic bite.
As my strong and neglected heart slackens its pace—

the house gone quiet save for human and animal
snores—I wish to remember, tomorrow, the slow,
measured motion of the blue whale, a mere
two heartbeats per minute as she dives,
sleek and magnificent and open-mouthed.

## Anthropocene Blessing: Snow Leopard

May the trail camera, perched
amid the Himalayan peaks,
capture only your haunches,
the ruddering twitch and sway
of your rosetted tail, as you
yellow the snow in a warding
spray of piss. May your kind
multiply and elude us,
accomplished in this game
of hide and seek, so thoroughly,
and for so long, that we leave off
our counting, abandon even
our calls of *here we come.*

## Anthropocene Blessing: Salt Creek Tiger Beetle

You with your sickled mandibles,
your quaternary lives. You who emerge
from the soft-bodied ground clacking
your predatory jaws, flashing your belly
of metallic green. You of the saline
wetlands. You of the tributary mud.
May the eggs you bury one by one,
sown in the salty earth like larval
seeds, hatch in an abundance of tiny
arthropods and salt. May you hinge
your fine-haired, tarsied legs across
the spearscale in Nebraska's summer
heat. May the white-faced ibis watch
over you as it wades in the marshy seeps.
May your tiger-mouthed, antennaed
face steer you swiftly, work its dread
grasp. May your ball bearing eyes,
your patterned back, be more fearfully
symmetric than our levees, our channeled
streams. May your briny future burn bright.

# Fossil Record: Ammonite

Words nestled in the chambers of my brain, not
numbers, which refused to suture themselves to me,

my neurons tentacling after them, floating through
the murky deep. Though I did like geometry—a class

in which our teacher stood on his head to keep us rapt
as points turned to lines, curves ellipsed across the page.

But calculus nearly did me in, and formulas in college
science labs spiraled me back to the buoyancy of language,

grammar re-shelling me in the coils of its arms. Until
the Fibonacci sequence awoke what I had let go dark:

the wonder of nature's mathematics, perfection of petals,
webs, and seeds. The golden ratio radiates through

siphuncle and septa as ammonoid bodies surface across
glaciers and plains. Once abundant in all of Earth's oceans,

defying three extinctions before their meteoric end, they've never
needed us to name them, date them, index their molluskan forms.

But I needed to explode my mind around their mineral sums:
my world expanding further and further, beyond measure.

# Riding the Ichthyosaur
### after Mary Anning

The fish lizard rises through a cliff bed
as her linen pouch of stone bones clatters:
devil's fingers, snake-stones, verteberries
clack their fossil bodies, shift and slide.

Her brother finds the skull—pointed jaw
and conical teeth—but she summons
the rest of the beast. Basket of torso, flippered
phalanges beneath the unsung fingers of a girl.

All those invisible years, I picture her riding
the sea dragon: one hand reining its skeletal
spine, the other gripping her crude extraction
tool. Plesiosaurs surface through Jurassic waves,

Pterodactyls circle her on bony wings. She dodges
lightning, drags Darwin along in her wake.
In the churchyard, her ghost saddles up. Splinters
the stones to expose both monsters and men.

# Anthropocene Blessing: Marine Iguana

Blunt-snouted one, basking
your crested spine, your
copper-mottled hide, in
the Galapagos heat. Salt
sneezer, algae eater,
long-clawed lava clinger.
May your soil-nested
eggs be safe from alien
dogs. May oil never
slick your tidal zones.
May all who crawl upon
you—lava lizards, crabs,
mockingbirds and finches,
fish who clean your
molting skin—be ever
nourished. As the ocean
rises, may it deter we who
invade with our pathogens
and tourist hands. May
your saltwater colonies
lounge in warm heaps
on the rocks, coexist
with the calescent sun.

## Anthropocene Blessing: Polar Bear

Nanook of many names—ice
bear, white bear, maritime bear—
still-hunting in your broken,
floating home, when the breath
of each seal wafts across your
patient, black-buttoned snout,
stirs your titanic forepaws
to the heave and kill, may you
feast and ensanguine the sea ice.
May the crimson spoils not
be metaphor, not stand in
for the way your opalescent
world recedes as you rotate
each skull, globelike, before
the rubbling crush of your jaws.

# Vaulted Seeds

*after the Svalbard Global Seed Vault*


Hoarded at the heart of an Arctic mountain,
within an archipelago of snow: an ark of seeds.
Cocooned against soil, nuclear bodies hunker
and wait for some future hungerscape. A gathering

of crops, varied faces folded into foil,
shuttered from the earth. Lentil, dark and round
and pebble-smooth. Barley's slender husk of an eye.
Each wrinkled chickpea the embryonic head of a bird.

Sister seeds, in Aleppo, shelter abandoned
in the rubble of war. The snow is a silence
except for how the seeds call out to one another
across land masses that shift and warm.

Svalbard reindeer swivel their ears to listen.
Foxes pause ghostlike on the permafrost. With one
quadrate eye, the vault reflects a frigid blue sea.
Ringed seals bob and dive among the glassy floes.

The vault's stone hull juts like a shipwreck in the drifted
ice while polar bears chuff and lumber past the door.
Inside, thousands upon thousands of promises to feed
what may remain. Doomsday, its other name.

Because we've already planted what's to come.

## Miraculous

When all the news is bad or worse, my ears
ringing like a din of night insects—just swelter

and drone—I quiet my bones with the thought
of quaking aspen. Trembling Giant: grove

of thousands of trees, all with a single system
of roots. A million years old, bright fluttering

of gold against blue. And when I think I can't
take in another sorrow—each a stone stacked

up like a cairn on my heart—I remember how
the jaws of a snake unhinge. Its mouth opens

and opens to enfold what's impossibly large,
patient swallowing followed by a length

of rest. And when what we've done can't be
undone, hope just a speck on the future's

woolly back, I jumpstart my wonder with this:
the snow in Antarctica is sprinkled with the dust

of ancient stars. While we hunted and gathered,
the galaxy glittered and lay itself down in our light.

# Whale Fall

The ocean's innumerable tiny mouths
await the muffled impact like baby birds.
Sediment clouds up at the deadened

settling, and the flesh is set upon. How
the weight of loss can be beautiful
in its opening. Luminous worms undulate

like party streamers as isopods
and lobsters arrive to feast. This body
holds an ecosystem unto itself: species

found nowhere else but here, cleaved
to the sunken remains. Sleeper sharks
move in slow and gentle, ease

the messy carcass to gleaming bones.
And then, how the skeletal rafters
of grief fuzz and bloom. How sometimes

the coldest depths allow for such measured
undoing. All the while hungry lives
swarm and spread, come to stay.

Limpets attach to the unhidden core. Sorrow
in its abundance crushes, cycles, feeds.
How the body rests, rich in what sustains.

# Acknowledgments

My gratitude for residencies at The Mineral School in Mineral, Washington, and PLAYA in Summer Lake, Oregon, which gave me the focused time and space to work on the earliest of these poems.

Many of the poems in this collection would not exist without the wildly inventive writing prompts from Kelli Russell Agodon and Annette Spaulding-Convy of Two Sylvias Press. If you are a poet who challenged yourself with their advent calendar from December 2020, I hope you enjoy figuring out which of these poems were inspired by those prompts.

My heartfelt thanks to Catie Bull, Lisa Oliver, Jeremy Trabue, and Wally Schaefer for their insightful comments while I worked on these poems. My thanks, as well, to the poets of the annual December poetry blog organized by Laura Passin, whose encouragement over the course of two seasons helped bring these poems into the world.

And, of course, to my family, who made sure I had quiet and a room of my own in which to write, even while we hunkered down at home during a pandemic. You are my heart.

With deep thanks to the following publications in which some of the poems in this collection first appeared, sometimes in slightly different versions:

*About Place Journal*: "Anthropocene Blessing: Monarch Butterfly," "Anthropocene Blessing: Snow Leopard," "New Year's Eve in the Anthropause"

Academy of American Poets Poem-a-Day: "Vanishing"

*Alluvian:* "Carpe Diem"

*American Poetry Journal:* "Anthropocene Blessing: Orangutan"

*Book of Matches:* "Doraphobia," "Os Sacrum"

*Broadsided Press:* "Fossil Record: Smilodon"

*Clade Song*: "Canis," "Clothesline for the Sixth Extinction," "The Ghost of Marlin Perkins Visits Me Wearing a Copperhead"

*Crow & Cross Keys*: "Peatland Aisling," "Riding the Ichthyosaur"

*Feral: A Journal of Poetry and Art*: "Iteration"

*Inkwell Journal:* "Proof"

*Magma*: "Anthropocene Blessing: Sumatran Tiger"

*Menacing Hedge:* "En Plein Air," "Triolet for the Marine Biologist I Didn't Become"

*Monday Night:* "Laika," "Oasis"

*New American Writing*: "Dogs of Chernobyl"

*Rogue Agent:* "Age Old"

*Salamander:* "My Eco-Anxiety and Solastalgia Have It Out"

*Scientific American:* "Vaulted Seeds"

*Shooter Literary Magazine:* "Anthropocene Blessing: Giant Panda," "Anthropocene Blessing: Marine Iguana"

*Sky Island Journal:* "The Strip Mall Changes Its Mind"

*The Sonora Review:* "Kulning"

*Stirring: A Literary Collection:* "Fossil Record: Dimetrodon"

*SWIMM Every Day:* "Miraculous"

*Thalia:* "Whale Fall"

*The Tiger Moth Review:* "Anthropocene Blessing: Baobab," "Anthropocene Blessing: California Condor"

*Tiny Spoon:* "Anthropocene Blessing: Ghost Orchid"

*The Timberline Review:* "Fear of Grasshoppers," "Horse-Girl"

*Triggerfish Critical Review:* "Anthropocene Blessing: Corpse Flower"

*Watershed Review:* "Elegy for One Billion Animals," "L'Appel du Vide"

*West Trestle Review:* "Slow Living"

*Whale Road Review:* "Opossum Nocturne"

*The Wild Word:* "The Last Two Northern White Rhinos Discuss the Birds and the Bees," "Orion in the Oregon Outback," "Rabbit, Rabbit, Rabbit"

*The Worcester Review:* "Cephalopods Have Three Hearts"

*Word and Image 2018:* "Crow Opus"

**JACKLEG PRESS**

V. Joshua Adams, Scott Shibuya Brown, Brian Rivka Clifton, Brittney Corrigan, Jessica Cuello, Barbara Cully, Alison Cundiff, Suzanne Frischkorn, Victoria Garza, Reginald Gibbons, D.C. Gonzales-Prieto, Neil de la Flor, Joachim Glage, Caroline Goodwin, Kathryn Kruse, Meagan Lehr, Brigitte Lewis, Jean McGarry, D.K. McCutchen, Jenny Magnus, Rita Mookerjee, Mamie Morgan, Karen Rigby, cin salach, Jo Salas, Maureen Seaton, Kristine Snodgrass, Cornelia Maude Spelman, Peter Stenson, Melissa Studdard, Curious Theatre, Gemini Wahhaj, Megan Weiler, David Wesley Williams

jacklegpress.org

CPSIA information can be obtained
at www.ICGtesting.com
Printed in the USA
JSHW081920140623
43249JS00003B/176

9 781737 513483